TAO TEH
CHING

LAO TZU

TAO TEH CHING

Translated by
JOHN C. H. WU

SHAMBHALA
Boston & London
1990

Shambhala Publications, Inc.
Horticultural Hall
300 Massachusetts Avenue
Boston, Massachusetts 02115

12   11   10   9   8

Printed in Hong Kong on acid-free paper ⊗
Distributed in the United States by
Random House, Inc., and in Canada by
Random House of Canada Ltd

Cover art: *The Nine Dragons* (detail), by Chen Jung,
1244 C.E. (Sung period), Francis Gardner Curtis Fund,
courtesy of the Museum of Fine Arts, Boston.

ISBN 0-87773-542-5
LC 90-52692

See page 116 for
Library of Congress
Cataloging-in-Publication data.

I

Tao can be talked about, but not the Eternal Tao.

Names can be named, but not the Eternal Name.

As the origin of heaven-and-earth, it is nameless:

As "the Mother" of all things, it is nameable.

So, as ever hidden, we should look at its inner essence:

As always manifest, we should look at its outer aspects.

These two flow from the same source, though differently named;

And both are called mysteries.

The Mystery of mysteries is the Door of all essence.

2

When all the world recognizes beauty as
  beauty, this in itself is ugliness.
When all the world recognizes good as
  good, this in itself is evil.
Indeed, the hidden and the manifest give
  birth to each other.
Difficult and easy complement each
  other.
Long and short exhibit each other.
High and low set measure to each other.
Voice and sound harmonize each other.
Back and front follow each other.

Therefore, the Sage manages his affairs
  without ado,
And spreads his teaching without
  talking.
He denies nothing to the teeming things.

He rears them, but lays no claim to them.

He does his work, but sets no store by it.

He accomplishes his task, but does not dwell upon it.

And yet it is just because he does not dwell on it

That nobody can ever take it away from him.

3

By not exalting the talented you will cause the people to cease from rivalry and contention.

By not prizing goods hard to get, you will cause the people to cease from robbing and stealing.

By not displaying what is desirable, you will cause the people's hearts to remain undisturbed.

Therefore, the Sage's way of governing begins by

> Emptying the heart of desires,
> Filling the belly with food,
> Weakening the ambitions,
> Toughening the bones.

In this way he will cause the people to remain without knowledge and with-

out desire, and prevent the knowing
ones from any ado.
Practice Non-Ado, and everything will be
in order.

4

The Tao is like an empty bowl,
Which in being used can never be filled
    up.
Fathomless, it seems to be the origin of
    all things.
It blunts all sharp edges,
It unties all tangles,
It harmonizes all lights,
It unites the world into one whole.
Hidden in the deeps,
Yet it seems to exist forever.
I do not know whose child it is;
It seems to be the common ancestor of
    all, the father of things.

5

Heaven-and-Earth is not sentimental;
It treats all things as straw-dogs.
The Sage is not sentimental;
He treats all his people as straw-dogs.

Between Heaven and Earth,
There seems to be a Bellows:
It is empty, and yet it is inexhaustible;
The more it works, the more comes out
   of it.
No amount of words can fathom it:
Better look for it within you.

6

The Spirit of the Fountain dies not.
It is called the Mysterious Feminine.
The Doorway of the Mysterious
    Feminine
Is called the Root of Heaven-and-Earth.
Lingering like gossamer, it has only a
    hint of existence;
And yet when you draw upon it, it is
    inexhaustible.

7

Heaven lasts long, and Earth abides.
What is the secret of their durability?
Is it not because they do not live for
    themselves
That they can live so long?
Therefore, the Sage wants to remain
    behind,
But finds himself at the head of others;
Reckons himself out,
But finds himself safe and secure.
Is it not because he is selfless
That his Self is realized?

8

The highest form of goodness is like water.

Water knows how to benefit all things without striving with them.

It stays in places loathed by all men.

Therefore, it comes near the Tao.

In choosing your dwelling, know how to keep to the ground.

In cultivating your mind, know how to dive in the hidden deeps.

In dealing with others, know how to be gentle and kind.

In speaking, know how to keep your words.

In governing, know how to maintain order.

In transacting business, know how to be efficient.

In making a move, know how to choose
the right moment.
If you do not strive with others,
You will be free from blame.

9

As for holding to fullness,
Far better were it to stop in time!
Keep on beating and sharpening a sword,
And the edge cannot be preserved for
long.
Fill your house with gold and jade,
And it can no longer be guarded.
Set store by your riches and honour,
And you will only reap a crop of
calamities.
Here is the Way of Heaven:
When you have done your work, retire!

TAO TEH
CHING

10

In keeping the spirit and the vital soul together,
Are you able to maintain their perfect harmony?
In gathering your vital energy to attain suppleness,
Have you reached the state of a new-born babe?
In washing and clearing your inner vision,
Have you purified it of all dross?
In loving your people and governing your state,
Are you able to dispense with cleverness?
In the opening and shutting of heaven's gate,
Are you able to play the feminine part?

Enlightened and seeing far into all
 directions,
Can you at the same time remain de-
 tached and non-active?
Rear your people!
Feed your people!
Rear them without claiming them for
 your own!
Do your work without setting any store
 by it!
Be a leader, not a butcher!
This is called hidden Virtue.

11

Thirty spokes converge upon a single
hub;
It is on the hole in the center that the
use of the cart hinges.
We make a vessel from a lump of clay;
It is the empty space within the vessel
that makes it useful.
We make doors and windows for a room;
But it is these empty spaces that make
the room livable.
Thus, while the tangible has advantages,
It is the intangible that makes it useful.

12

The five colours blind the eye.
The five tones deafen the ear.
The five flavours cloy the palate.
Racing and hunting madden the mind.
Rare goods tempt men to do wrong.
Therefore, the Sage takes care of the
  belly, not the eye.
He prefers what is within to what is
  without.

Greatest frustration comes
from what you want

The box is more fun than
the toy

13

"Welcome disgrace as a pleasant
    surprise.
Prize calamities as your own body."
Why should we "welcome disgrace as a
    pleasant surprise"?
Because a lowly state is a boon:
Getting it is a pleasant surprise,
And so is losing it!
That is why we should "welcome dis-
grace as a pleasant surprise."
Why should we "prize calamities as our
    own body"?
Because our body is the very source of
    our calamities.
If we have no body, what calamities can
    we have?

Hence, only he who is willing to give his
body for the sake of the world is fit to
be entrusted with the world.
Only he who can do it with love is wor-
thy of being the steward of the world.

14

Look at it but you cannot see it!
Its name is *Formless*.

Listen to it but you cannot hear it!
Its name is *Soundless*.

Grasp it but you cannot get it!
Its name is *Incorporeal*.

These three attributes are unfathomable;
Therefore they fuse into one.

Its upper side is not bright:
Its under side not dim.

Continually the Unnameable moves on,
Until it returns beyond the realm of
    things.

We call it the formless Form, the image-
    less Image.

We call it the indefinable and
    unimaginable.

Confront it and you do not see its face!
Follow it and you do not see its back!
Yet, equipped with this timeless Tao,
You can harness present realities.
To know the origins is initiation into
  the Tao.

15

The ancient adepts of the Tao were sub-
   tle and flexible, profound and
   comprehensive.
Their minds were too deep to be
   fathomed.
Because they are unfathomable,
One can only describe them vaguely by
   their appearance.
Hesitant like one wading a stream in
   winter;
Timid like one afraid of his neighbours
   on all sides;
Cautious and courteous like a guest;
Yielding like ice on the point of melting;
Simple like an uncarved block;
Hollow like a cave;
Confused like a muddy pool;

And yet who else could quietly and grad-
    ually evolve from the muddy to the
    clear?
Who else could slowly but steadily move
    from the inert to the living?
He who keeps the Tao does not want to
    be full.
But precisely because he is never full,
He can always remain like a hidden
    sprout,
And does not rush to early ripening.

16

Attain to utmost Emptiness.
Cling single-heartedly to interior peace.
While all things are stirring together,
I only contemplate the Return.
For flourishing as they do,
Each of them will return to its root.
To return to the root is to find peace.
To find peace is to fulfill one's destiny.
To fulfill one's destiny is to be constant.
To know the Constant is called Insight.

If one does not know the Constant,
One runs blindly into disasters.
If one knows the Constant,
One can understand and embrace all.
If one understands and embraces all,
One is capable of doing justice.
To be just is to be kingly;
To be kingly is to be heavenly;

To be heavenly is to be one with the Tao;
To be one with the Tao is to abide
    forever.
Such a one will be safe and whole
Even after the dissolution of his body.

17

The highest type of ruler is one of whose
  existence the people are barely aware.
Next comes one whom they love and
  praise.
Next comes one whom they fear.
Next comes one whom they despise and
  defy.

When you are lacking in faith,
Others will be unfaithful to you.

The Sage is self-effacing and scanty of
  words.
When his task is accomplished and
  things have been completed,
All the people say, "We ourselves have
  achieved it!"

18

When the Great Tao was abandoned,
There appeared humanity and justice.
When intelligence and wit arose,
There appeared great hypocrites.
When the six relations lost their
    harmony,
There appeared filial piety and paternal
    kindness.
When darkness and disorder began to
    reign in a kingdom,
There appeared the loyal ministers.

19

Drop wisdom, abandon cleverness,
And the people will be benefited a
hundredfold.

Drop humanity, abandon justice,
And the people will return to their natural affections.

Drop shrewdness, abandon sharpness,
And robbers and thieves will cease to be.

These three are the criss-cross of Tao,
And are not sufficient in themselves.
Therefore, they should be subordinated
To a Higher principle:
See the Simple and embrace the Primal,
Diminish the self and curb the desires!

20

Have done with learning,
And you will have no more vexation.
How great is the difference between
   "eh" and "o"?
What is the distinction between "good"
   and "evil"?
Must I fear what others fear?
What abysmal nonsense this is!

All men are joyous and beaming,
As though feasting upon a sacrificial ox,
As though mounting the Spring Terrace;
I alone am placid and give no sign,
Like a babe which has not yet smiled.
I alone am forlorn as one who has no
   home to return to.

All men have enough and to spare:
I alone appear to possess nothing.
What a fool I am!

What a muddled mind I have!
All men are bright, bright:
I alone am dim, dim.
All men are sharp, sharp:
I alone am mum, mum!
Bland like the ocean,
Aimless like the wafting gale.
All men settle down in their grooves:
I alone am stubborn and remain outside.
But wherein I am most different from
    others is
In knowing to take sustenance from my
    Mother!

21

It lies in the nature of Grand Virtue
To follow the Tao and the Tao alone.
Now what is the Tao?
It is Something elusive and evasive.
Evasive and elusive!
And yet It contains within Itself a Form.
  Elusive and evasive!
And yet It contains within Itself a
  Substance.
Shadowy and dim!
And yet It contains within Itself a Core
  of Vitality.
The Core of Vitality is very real,
It contains within Itself an unfailing
  Sincerity.
Throughout the ages Its Name has been
  preserved

In order to recall the Beginning of all
   things.
How do I know the ways of all things at
   the Beginning?
By what is within me.

22

Bend and you will be whole.
Curl and you will be straight.
Keep empty and you will be filled.
Grow old and you will be renewed.

Have little and you will gain.
Have much and you will be confused.

Therefore, the Sage embraces the One,
And becomes a Pattern to all under
    Heaven.
He does not make a show of himself,
Hence he shines;
Does not justify himself,
Hence he becomes known;
Does not boast of his ability,
Hence he gets his credit;
Does not brandish his success,
Hence he endures;
Does not compete with anyone,

Hence no one can compete with him.
Indeed, the ancient saying: "Bend and
  you will remain whole" is no idle
  word.
Nay, if you have really attained wholeness, everything will flock to you.

23

Only simple and quiet words will ripen
   of themselves.
For a whirlwind does not last a whole
   morning,
Nor does a sudden shower last a whole
   day.
Who is their author? Heaven-and-Earth!
Even Heaven-and-Earth cannot make
   such violent things last long;
How much truer is it of the rash endeav-
   ours of men?

Hence, he who cultivates the Tao is one
   with the Tao;
He who practices Virtue is one with
   Virtue;
And he who courts after Loss is one with
   Loss.

To be one with the Tao is to be a wel-
    come accession to the Tao;
To be one with Virtue is to be a welcome
    accession to Virtue;
To be one with Loss is to be a welcome
    accession to Loss.

Deficiency of faith on your part
Entails faithlessness on the part of
    others.

24

One on tip-toe cannot stand.
One astride cannot walk.
One who displays himself does not shine.
One who justifies himself has no glory.
One who boasts of his own ability has no merit.
One who parades his own success will not endure.
In Tao these things are called "unwanted food and extraneous growths,"
Which are loathed by all things.
Hence, a man of Tao does not set his heart upon them.

25

There was Something undefined and yet
  complete in itself,
Born before Heaven-and-Earth.

Silent and boundless,
Standing alone without change,
Yet pervading all without fail,
It may be regarded as the Mother of the
  world.
I do not know its name;
I style it "Tao";
And, in the absence of a better word, call
  it "The Great."

To be great is to go on,
To go on is to be far,
To be far is to return.

Hence, "Tao is great,
Heaven is great,
Earth is great,

King is great."
Thus, the king is one of the great four in
    the Universe.

Man follows the ways of the Earth.
The Earth follows the ways of Heaven,
Heaven follows the ways of Tao,
Tao follows its own ways.

26

Heaviness is the root of lightness.
Serenity is the master of restlessness.

Therefore, the Sage, travelling all day,
Does not part with the baggage-wagon;
Though there may be gorgeous sights to
    see,
He stays at ease in his own home.
Why should a lord of ten thousand
    chariots
Display his lightness to the world?
To be light is to be separated from one's
    root;
To be restless is to lose one's self-
    mastery.

27

Good walking leaves no track behind it;
Good speech leaves no mark to be picked
    at;
Good calculation makes no use of count-
    ing-slips;
Good shutting makes no use of bolt and
    bar,
And yet nobody can undo it;
Good tying makes no use of rope and
    knot,
And yet nobody can untie it.
Hence, the Sage is always good at saving
    men,
And therefore nobody is abandoned;
Always good at saving things,
And therefore nothing is wasted.
This is called "following the guidance of
    the Inner Light."

Hence, good men are teachers of bad
    men,
While bad men are the charge of good
    men.
Not to revere one's teacher,
Not to cherish one's charge,
Is to be on the wrong road, however in-
    telligent one may be.
This is an essential tenet of the Tao.

28

Know the masculine,
Keep to the feminine,
And be the Brook of the World.
To be the Brook of the World is
To move constantly in the path of Virtue
Without swerving from it,
And to return again to infancy.

Know the white,
Keep to the black,
And be the Pattern of the World.
To be the Pattern of the World is
To move constantly in the path of Virtue
Without erring a single step,
And to return again to the Infinite.

Know the glorious,
Keep to the lowly,
And be the Fountain of the World.

To be the Fountain of the World is
To live the abundant life of Virtue,
And to return again to Primal Simplicity.

When Primal Simplicity diversifies,
It becomes useful vessels,
Which, in the hands of the Sage, become
    officers.

Hence, "a great tailor does little
    cutting."

29

Does anyone want to take the world and
do what he wants with it?

I do not see how he can succeed.

The world is a sacred vessel, which must
not be tampered with or grabbed
after.

To tamper with it is to spoil it, and to
grasp it is to lose it.

In fact, for all things there is a time for
going ahead, and a time for following
behind;

A time for slow-breathing and a time for
fast-breathing;

A time to grow in strength and a time to
decay;

A time to be up and a time to be down.

Therefore, the Sage avoids all extremes,
excesses and extravagances.

30

He who knows how to guide a ruler in
  the path of Tao
Does not try to override the world with
  force of arms.
It is in the nature of a military weapon
  to turn against its wielder.
Wherever armies are stationed, thorny
  bushes grow.
After a great war, bad years invariably
  follow.
What you want is to protect efficiently
  your own state,
But not to aim at self-aggrandisement.
After you have attained your purpose,
You must not parade your success,
You must not boast of your ability,
You must not feel proud,

You must rather regret that you had not
   been able to prevent the war.

You must never think of conquering others by force.

For to be over-developed is to hasten
   decay,

And this is against Tao,

And what is against Tao will soon cease
   to be.

31

Fine weapons of war augur evil.
Even things seem to hate them.
Therefore, a man of Tao does not set his
  heart upon them.
In ordinary life, a gentleman regards the
  left side as the place of honour:
In war, the right side is the place of
  honour.
As weapons are instruments of evil,
They are not properly a gentleman's
  instruments;
Only on necessity will he resort to them.
For peace and quiet are dearest to his
  heart,
And to him even a victory is no cause for
  rejoicing.
To rejoice over a victory is to rejoice over
  the slaughter of men!

Hence a man who rejoices over the slaughter of men cannot expect to thrive in the world of men.

On happy occasions the left side is preferred:

On sad occasions the right side.

In the army, the Lieutenant Commander stands on the left,

While the Commander-in-Chief stands on the right.

This means that war is treated on a par with a funeral service.

Because many people have been killed, it is only right that survivors should mourn for them.

Hence, even a victory is a funeral.

32

Tao is always nameless.
Small as it is in its Primal Simplicity,
It is inferior to nothing in the world.
If only a ruler could cling to it,
Everything will render homage to him.
Heaven and Earth will be harmonized
And send down sweet dew.
Peace and order will reign among the
    people
Without any command from above.
When once the Primal Simplicity
    diversified,
Different names appeared.
Are there not enough names now?

Is this not the time to stop?
To know when to stop is to preserve
    ourselves from danger.
The Tao is to the world what a great
    river or an ocean is to the streams and
    brooks.

33

He who knows men is clever;
He who knows himself has insight.
He who conquers men has force;
He who conquers himself is truly strong.
He who knows when he has got enough
    is rich,
And he who adheres assiduously to the
    path of Tao is a man of steady
    purpose.
He who stays where he has found his
    true home endures long,
And he who dies but perishes not enjoys
    real longevity.

34

The Great Tao is universal like a flood.
How can it be turned to the right or to
  the left?
All creatures depend on it,
And it denies nothing to anyone.
It does its work,
But it makes no claims for itself.
It clothes and feeds all,
But it does not lord it over them:
Thus, it may be called "the Little."
All things return to it as to their home,
But it does not lord it over them:
Thus, it may be called "the Great."
It is just because it does not wish to be
  great
That its greatness is fully realized.

35

He who holds the Great Symbol will
  attract all things to him.
They flock to him and receive no harm,
  for in him they find peace, security
  and happiness.
Music and dainty dishes can only make a
  passing guest pause.
But the words of Tao possess lasting
  effects,
Though they are mild and flavourless,
Though they appeal neither to the eye
  nor to the ear.

36

What is in the end to be shrunken,
Begins by being first stretched out.
What is in the end to be weakened,
Begins by being first made strong.
What is in the end to be thrown down,
Begins by being first set on high.
What is in the end to be despoiled,
Begins by being first richly endowed.
Herein is the subtle wisdom of life:
The soft and weak overcomes the hard
    and strong.
Just as the fish must not leave the deeps,
So the ruler must not display his
    weapons.

37

Tao never makes any ado,
And yet it does everything.
If a ruler can cling to it,
All things will grow of themselves.
When they have grown and tend to make
  a stir,
It is time to keep them in their place by
  the aid of the nameless Primal
  Simplicity,
Which alone can curb the desires of
  men.
When the desires of men are curbed,
  there will be peace,
And the world will settle down of its
  own accord.

38

High Virtue is non-virtuous;
Therefore it has Virtue.
Low Virtue never frees itself from
   virtuousness;
Therefore it has no Virtue.
High Virtue makes no fuss and has no
   private ends to serve:
Low Virtue not only fusses but has pri-
   vate ends to serve.
High humanity fusses but has no private
   ends to serve:
High morality not only fusses but has
   private ends to serve.
High ceremony fusses but finds no
   response;
Then it tries to enforce itself with rolled-
   up sleeves.

Failing Tao, man resorts to Virtue.

Failing Virtue, man resorts to humanity.

Failing humanity, man resorts to morality.

Failing morality, man resorts to ceremony.

Now, ceremony is the merest husk of faith and loyalty;

It is the beginning of all confusion and disorder.

As to foreknowledge, it is only the flower of Tao,

And the beginning of folly.

Therefore, the full-grown man sets his heart upon the substance rather than the husk;

Upon the fruit rather than the flower.

Truly, he prefers what is within to what is without.

39

From of old there are not lacking things
  that have attained Oneness.
The sky attained Oneness and became
  clear;
The earth attained Oneness and became
  calm;
The spirits attained Oneness and became
  charged with mystical powers;
The fountains attained Oneness and be-
  came full;
The ten thousand creatures attained
  Oneness and became reproductive;
Barons and princes attained Oneness and
  became sovereign rulers of the world.
All of them are what they are by virtue
  of Oneness.

If the sky were not clear, it would be
  likely to fall to pieces;

If the earth were not calm, it would be
likely to burst into bits;

If the spirits were not charged with mystical powers, they would be likely to
cease from being;

If the fountains were not full, they would
be likely to dry up;

If the ten thousand creatures were not
reproductive, they would be likely to
come to extinction;

If the barons and princes were not the
sovereign rulers, they would be likely
to stumble and fall.

Truly, humility is the root from which
greatness springs,

And the high must be built upon the
foundation of the low.

That is why barons and princes style
themselves "The Helpless One," "The
Little One," and "The Worthless
One."

Perhaps they too realize their dependence upon the lowly.

Truly, too much honour means no honour.

It is not wise to shine like jade and resound like stone-chimes.

40

The movement of the Tao consists in
  Returning.
The use of the Tao consists in softness.
All things under heaven are born of the
  corporeal:
The corporeal is born of the Incorporeal.

We all come from the same place
& all go to the same place

41

When a wise scholar hears the Tao,
He practices it diligently.
When a mediocre scholar hears the Tao,
He wavers between belief and unbelief.
When a worthless scholar hears the Tao,
He laughs boisterously at it.
But if such a one does not laugh at it,
The Tao would not be the Tao!

The wise men of old have truly said:

  The bright Way looks dim.
  The progressive Way looks retrograde.
  The smooth Way looks rugged.
  High Virtue looks like an abyss.
  Great whiteness looks spotted.
  Abundant Virtue looks deficient.
  Established Virtue looks shabby.
  Solid Virtue looks as though melted.
  Great squareness has no corners.

Great talents ripen late.
Great sound is silent.
Great Form is shapeless.
The Tao is hidden and nameless;
Yet it alone knows how to render help
    and to fulfill.

42

Tao gave birth to One,
One gave birth to Two,
Two gave birth to Three,
Three gave birth to all the myriad things.
All the myriad things carry the *Yin* on
  their backs and hold the *Yang* in their
  embrace,
Deriving their vital harmony from the
  proper blending of the two vital
  Breaths.
What is more loathed by men than to be
  "helpless," "little," and "worthless"?
And yet these are the very names the
  princes and barons call themselves.
Truly, one may gain by losing;
And one may lose by gaining.

What another has taught let me repeat:
"A man of violence will come to a vio-
    lent end."
Whoever said this can be my teacher and
    my father.

43

The softest of all things
Overrides the hardest of all things.
Only Nothing can enter into no-space.
Hence I know the advantages of Non-
    Ado.
Few things under heaven are as instruc-
    tive as the lessons of Silence,
Or as beneficial as the fruits of Non-Ado.

44

As for your name and your body, which is the dearer?

As for your body and your wealth, which is the more to be prized?

As for gain and loss, which is the more painful?

Thus, an excessive love for anything will cost you dear in the end.

The storing up of too much goods will entail a heavy loss.

To know when you have enough is to be immune from disgrace.

To know when to stop is to be preserved from perils.

Only thus can you endure long.

45

The greatest perfection seems imperfect,
And yet its use is inexhaustible.
The greatest fullness seems empty,
And yet its use is endless.
The greatest straightness looks like
    crookedness.
The greatest skill appears clumsy.
The greatest eloquence sounds like
    stammering.
Restlessness overcomes cold,
But calm overcomes heat.
The peaceful and serene
Is the Norm of the World.

46

When the world is in possession of the
  Tao,
The galloping horses are led to fertilize
  the fields with their droppings.
When the world has become Taoless,
War horses breed themselves on the
  suburbs.
There is no calamity like not knowing
  what is enough.
There is no evil like covetousness.
Only he who knows what is enough will
  always have enough.

47

Without going out of your door,
You can know the ways of the world.
Without peeping through your window,
You can see the Way of Heaven.
The farther you go,
The less you know.

Thus, the Sage knows without travelling,
Sees without looking,
And achieves without Ado.

48

Learning consists in daily accumulating;
The practice of Tao consists in daily
   diminishing.
Keep on diminishing and diminishing,
Until you reach the state of No-Ado.
No-Ado, and yet nothing is left undone.
To win the world, one must renounce all.
If one still has private ends to serve,
One will never be able to win the world.

49

The Sage has no interests of his own,
But takes the interests of the people as
 his own.
He is kind to the kind;
He is also kind to the unkind:
For Virtue is kind.
He is faithful to the faithful;
He is also faithful to the unfaithful:
For Virtue is faithful.
In the midst of the world, the Sage is shy
 and self-effacing.
For the sake of the world he keeps his
 heart in its nebulous state.
All the people strain their ears and eyes:
The Sage only smiles like an amused
 infant.

50

When one is out of Life, one is in Death. The companions of Life are thirteen; the companions of Death are thirteen; and, when a living person moves into the Realm of Death, his companions are also thirteen. How is this? Because he draws upon the resources of Life too heavily.

It is said that he who knows well how to live meets no tigers or wild buffaloes on his road, and comes out from the battle-ground untouched by the weapons of war. For, in him, a buffalo would find no butt for his horns, a tiger nothing to lay his claws upon, and a weapon of war no place to admit its point. How is this? Because there is no room for Death in him.

51

Tao gives them life,
Virtue nurses them,
Matter shapes them,
Environment perfects them.
Therefore all things without exception
    worship Tao and do homage to Virtue.
They have not been commanded to wor-
    ship Tao and do homage to Virtue,
But they always do so spontaneously.
It is Tao that gives them life:
It is Virtue that nurses them, grows
    them, fosters them, shelters them,
    comforts them, nourishes them, and
    covers them under her wings.
To give life but to claim nothing,
To do your work but to set no store by
    it,
To be a leader, not a butcher,
This is called hidden Virtue.

52

All-under-Heaven have a common
　　Beginning.
This Beginning is the Mother of the
　　world.
Having known the Mother,
We may proceed to know her children.
Having known the children,
We should go back and hold on to the
　　Mother.
In so doing, you will incur no risk
Even though your body be annihilated.
Block all the passages!
Shut all the doors!
And to the end of your days you will not
　　be worn out.
Open the passages!
Multiply your activities!

And to the end of your days you will
    remain helpless.

To see the small is to have insight.

To hold on to weakness is to be strong.

Use the lights, but return to your
    insight.

Do not bring calamities upon yourself.

This is the way of cultivating the
    Changeless.

53

If only I had the tiniest grain of wisdom,
I should walk in the Great Way,
And my only fear would be to stray from
   it.
The Great Way is very smooth and
   straight;
And yet the people prefer devious paths.
The court is very clean and well
   garnished,
But the fields are very weedy and wild,
And the granaries are very empty!
They wear gorgeous clothes,
They carry sharp swords,
They surfeit themselves with food and
   drink,
They possess more riches than they can
   use!
They are the heralds of brigandage!
As for Tao, what do they know about it?

54

What is well planted cannot be
  uprooted.
What is well embraced cannot slip away.
Your descendants will carry on the an-
  cestral sacrifice for generations without end.

Cultivate Virtue in your own person,
And it becomes a genuine part of you.
Cultivate it in the family,
And it will abide.
Cultivate it in the community,
And it will live and grow.
Cultivate it in the state,
And it will flourish abundantly.
Cultivate it in the world,
And it will become universal.

Hence, a person must be judged as
  person;

A family as family;
A community as community;
A state as state;
The world as world.
How do I know about the world?
By what is within me.

55

One who is steeped in Virtue is akin to
the new-born babe.
Wasps and poisonous serpents do not
sting it,
Nor fierce beasts seize it,
Nor birds of prey maul it.
Its bones are tender, its sinews soft,
But its grip is firm.
It has not known the union of the male
and the female,
Growing in its wholeness, and keeping
its vitality in its perfect integrity.
It howls and screams all day long without
getting hoarse,
Because it embodies perfect harmony.
To know harmony is to know the
Changeless.

To know the Changeless is to have
insight.

To hasten the growth of life is ominous.

To control the breath by the will is to
overstrain it.

To be overgrown is to decay.

All this is against Tao,

And whatever is against Tao soon ceases
to be.

56

He who knows does not speak.
He who speaks does not know.

Block all the passages!
Shut all the doors!
Blunt all edges!
Untie all tangles!
Harmonize all lights!
Unite the world into one whole!
This is called the Mystical Whole,
Which you cannot court after nor shun,
Benefit nor harm, honour nor humble.

Therefore, it is the Highest of the world.

57

You govern a kingdom by normal rules;
You fight a war by exceptional moves;
But you win the world by letting alone.
How do I know that this is so?
By what is within me!

The more taboos and inhibitions there
    are in the world,
The poorer the people become.
The sharper the weapons the people
    possess,
The greater confusion reigns in the
    realm.
The more clever and crafty the men,
The oftener strange things happen.
The more articulate the laws and
    ordinances,
The more robbers and thieves arise.

Therefore, the Sage says:
I do not make any fuss, and the people
    transform themselves.
I love quietude, and the people settle
    down in their regular grooves.
I do not engage myself in anything, and
    the people grow rich.
I have no desires, and the people return
    to Simplicity.

58

Where the ruler is mum, mum,
The people are simple and happy.
Where the ruler is sharp, sharp,
The people are wily and discontented.
Bad fortune is what good fortune leans
   on,
Good fortune is what bad fortune hides
   in.
Who knows the ultimate end of this
   process?
Is there no norm of right?
Yet what is normal soon becomes
   abnormal,
And what is auspicious soon turns
   ominous.
Long indeed have the people been in a
   quandary.

Therefore, the Sage squares without cutting, carves without disfiguring, straightens without straining, enlightens without dazzling.

59

In governing a people and in serving
  Heaven,
There is nothing like frugality.
To be frugal is to return before straying.
To return before straying is to have a
  double reserve of Virtue.
To have a double reserve of Virtue is to
  overcome everything.
To overcome everything is to reach an
  invisible height.
Only he who has reached an invisible
  height can have a kingdom.
Only he who has got the Mother of a
  kingdom can last long.
This is the way to be deep-rooted and
  firm-planted in the Tao.
The secret of long life and lasting vision.

60

Ruling a big kingdom is like cooking a small fish. When a man of Tao reigns over the world, demons have no spiritual powers. Not that the demons have no spiritual powers, but the spirits themselves do no harm to men. Not that the spirits do no harm to men, but the Sage himself does no harm to his people. If only the ruler and his people would refrain from harming each other, all the benefits of life would accumulate in the kingdom.

61

A great country is like the lowland toward which all streams flow. It is the Reservoir of all under heaven, the Feminine of the world.

The Feminine always conquers the Masculine by her quietness, by lowering herself through her quietness.

Hence, if a great country can lower itself before a small country, it will win over the small country; and if a small country can lower itself before a great country, it will win over the great country. The one wins by stooping; the other, by remaining low.

What a great country wants is simply to embrace more people; and what a small country wants is simply to come to serve its patron. Thus, each gets what it wants. But it behooves a great country to lower itself.

62

The Tao is the hidden Reservoir of all
    things.
A treasure to the honest, it is a safeguard
    to the erring.
A good word will find its own market.
A good deed may be used as a gift to
    another.
That a man is straying from the right
    path
Is no reason that he should be cast away.
Hence, at the Enthronement of an
    Emperor,
Or at the Installation of the Three
    Ministers,
Let others offer their discs of jade, fol-
    lowing it up with teams of horses;
It is better for you to offer the Tao with-
    out moving your feet!

Why did the ancients prize the Tao?
Is it not because by virtue of it he who
    seeks finds,
And the guilty are forgiven?
That is why it is such a treasure to the
    world.

63

Do the Non-Ado.
Strive for the effortless.
Savour the savourless.
Exalt the low.
Multiply the few.
Requite injury with kindness.
Nip troubles in the bud.
Sow the great in the small.
Difficult things of the world
Can only be tackled when they are easy.
Big things of the world
Can only be achieved by attending to
    their small beginnings.
Thus, the Sage never has to grapple with
    big things,
Yet he alone is capable of achieving them!
He who promises lightly must be lacking
    in faith.

He who thinks everything easy will end
    by finding everything difficult.
Therefore, the Sage, who regards every-
    thing as difficult,
Meets with no difficulties in the end.

64

What is at rest is easy to hold.
What manifests no omens is easily
    forestalled.
What is fragile is easily shattered.
What is small is easily scattered.
Tackle things before they have appeared.
Cultivate peace and order before confu-
    sion and disorder have set in.
A tree as big as a man's embrace springs
    from a tiny sprout.
A tower nine stories high begins with a
    heap of earth.
A journey of a thousand leagues starts
    from where your feet stand.
He who fusses over anything spoils it.
He who grasps anything loses it.
The Sage fusses over nothing and there-
    fore spoils nothing.

He grips at nothing and therefore loses
nothing.
In handling affairs, people often spoil
them just at the point of success.
With heedfulness in the beginning and
patience at the end, nothing will be
spoiled.
Therefore, the Sage desires to be
desireless,
Sets no value on rare goods,
Learns to unlearn his learning,
And induces the masses to return from
where they have overpassed.
He only helps all creatures to find their
own nature,
But does not venture to lead them by the
nose.

65

In the old days, those who were well versed in the practice of the Tao did not try to enlighten the people, but rather to keep them in the state of simplicity. For, why are the people hard to govern? Because they are too clever! Therefore, he who governs his state with cleverness is its malefactor; but he who governs his state without resorting to cleverness is its benefactor. To know these principles is to possess a rule and a measure. To keep the rule and the measure constantly in your mind is what we call Mystical Virtue. Deep and far-reaching is Mystical Virtue! It leads all things to return, till they come back to Great Harmony!

66

How does the sea become the king of all
  streams?
Because it lies lower than they!
Hence it is the king of all streams.

Therefore, the Sage reigns over the people by humbling himself in speech;
And leads the people by putting himself
  behind.

Thus it is that when a Sage stands above
  the people, they do not feel the heaviness of his weight;
And when he stands in front of the people, they do not feel hurt.

Therefore all the world is glad to push
  him forward without getting tired of
  him.

Just because he strives with nobody,
Nobody can ever strive with him.

67

All the world says that my Tao is great, but seems queer, like nothing on earth. But it is just because my Tao is great that it is like nothing on earth! If it were like anything on earth, how small it would have been from the very beginning!

I have Three Treasures, which I hold fast and watch over closely. The first is *Mercy*. The second is *Frugality*. The third is *Not Daring to Be First in the World*. Because I am merciful, therefore I can be brave. Because I am frugal, therefore I can be generous. Because I dare not be first, therefore I can be the chief of all vessels.

If a man wants to be brave without first being merciful, generous without first being frugal, a leader without first wishing to follow, he is only courting death!

Mercy alone can help you to win a war. Mercy alone can help you to defend your state. For Heaven will come to the rescue of the merciful, and protect him with *its* Mercy.

68

A good soldier is never aggressive;
A good fighter is never angry.
The best way of conquering an enemy
Is to win him over by not antagonizing
    him.
The best way of employing a man
Is to serve under him.
This is called the virtue of non-striving!
This is called using the abilities of men!
This is called being wedded to Heaven as
    of old!

69

The strategists have a saying:
I dare not be a host, but rather a guest;
I dare not advance an inch, but rather
retreat a foot.

This is called marching without moving,
Rolling up one's sleeves without baring
one's arms,
Capturing the enemy without confront-
ing him,
Holding a weapon that is invisible.

There is no greater calamity than to under-estimate the strength of your
enemy.
For to under-estimate the strength of
your enemy is to lose your treasure.

Therefore, when opposing troops meet
in battle, victory belongs to the griev-
ing side.

70

My words are very easy to understand,
   and very easy to practise:
But the world cannot understand them,
   nor practise them.

My words have an Ancestor.
My deeds have a Lord.
The people have no knowledge of this.
Therefore, they have no knowledge of
   me.

The fewer persons know me,
The nobler are they that follow me.
Therefore, the Sage wears coarse clothes,
While keeping the jade in his bosom.

71

To realize that our knowledge is
    ignorance,
This is a noble insight.
To regard our ignorance as knowledge,
This is mental sickness.
Only when we are sick of our sickness
Shall we cease to be sick.
The Sage is not sick, being sick of
    sickness;
This is the secret of health.

72

When the people no longer fear your
  power,
It is a sign that a greater power is
  coming.
Interfere not lightly with their dwelling,
Nor lay heavy burdens upon their
  livelihood.
Only when you cease to weary them,
They will cease to be wearied of you.
Therefore, the Sage knows himself,
But makes no show of himself;
Loves himself,
But does not exalt himself.
He prefers what is within to what is
  without.

73

He who is brave in daring will be killed;
He who is brave in not daring will
survive.
Of these two kinds of bravery, one is
beneficial, while the other proves
harmful.
Some things are detested by Heaven,
But who knows the reason?
Even the Sage is baffled by such a
question.
It is Heaven's Way to conquer without
striving,
To get responses without speaking,
To induce the people to come without
summoning,
To act according to plans without haste.
Vast is Heaven's net;
Sparse-meshed it is, and yet
Nothing can slip through it.

74

When the people are no longer afraid of
    death,
Why scare them with the spectre of
    death?
If you could make the people always
    afraid of death,
And they still persisted in breaking the
    law,
Then you might with reason arrest and
    execute them,
And who would dare to break the law?
Is not the Great Executor always there
    to kill?
To do the killing for the Great Executor
Is to chop wood for a master carpenter,
And you would be lucky indeed if you
    did not hurt your own hand!

75

Why are the people starving?
Because those above them are taxing
    them too heavily.
That is why they are starving.
Why are the people hard to manage?
Because those above them are fussy and
    have private ends to serve.
That is why they are hard to manage.
Why do the people make light of death?
Because those above them make too
    much of life.
That is why they make light of death.

The people have simply nothing to live
    upon!
They know better than to value such a
    life!

76

When a man is living, he is soft and
  supple.
When he is dead, he becomes hard and
  rigid.
When a plant is living, it is soft and
  tender.
When it is dead, it becomes withered
  and dry.
Hence, the hard and rigid belongs to the
  company of the dead:
The soft and supple belongs to the com-
  pany of the living.
Therefore, a mighty army tends to fall by
  its own weight,
Just as dry wood is ready for the axe.
The mighty and great will be laid low;
The humble and weak will be exalted.

77

Perhaps the Way of Heaven may be likened to the stretching of a composite bow! The upper part is depressed, while the lower is raised. If the bow-string is too long, it is cut short: if too short, it is added to.

The Way of Heaven diminishes the more-than-enough to supply the less-than-enough. The way of man is different: it takes from the less-than-enough to swell the more-than-enough. Who except a man of the Tao can put his superabundant riches to the service of the world?

Therefore, the Sage does his work without setting any store by it, accomplishes his task without dwelling upon it. He does not want his merits to be seen.

78

Nothing in the world is softer and
  weaker than water;
But, for attacking the hard and strong,
  there is nothing like it!
For nothing can takes its place.
That the weak overcomes the strong, and
  the soft overcomes the hard,
This is something known by all, but
  practised by none.
Therefore, the Sage says:
To receive the dirt of a country is to be
  the lord of its soil-shrines.
To bear the calamities of a country is to
  be the prince of the world.
Indeed, Truth sounds like its opposite!

79

When a great wound is healed,
There will still remain a scar.
Can this be a desirable state of affairs?
Therefore, the Sage, holding the left-
  hand tally,
Performs his part of the covenant,
But lays no claims upon others.

The virtuous attends to his duties;
The virtueless knows only to levy duties
  upon the people.
The Way of Heaven has no private
  affections,
But always accords with the good.

80

Ah, for a small country with a small population! Though there are highly efficient mechanical contrivances, the people have no use for them. Let them mind death and refrain from migrating to distant places. Boats and carriages, weapons and armour there may still be, but there are no occasions for using or displaying them. Let the people revert to communication by knotting cords. See to it that they are contented with their food, pleased with their clothing, satisfied with their houses, and inured to their simple ways of living. Though there may be another country in the neighbourhood so close that they are within sight of each other and the crowing of cocks and barking of dogs in one place can be heard in the other, yet there is no traffic between them, and throughout their lives the two peoples have nothing to do with each other.